D0427349

SISKIYOU COUNTY SCHOOLS
SCIENCE PROJECT

SISKIYOU COUNTY SCHOOLS
SCIENCE PROJECT

Farms

SISKIYOU COUNTY SCHOOLS
SCIENCE PROJECT

WONDER
STARTERS

Farms

Pictures by ESME EVE

Published by WONDER BOOKS
A Division of Grosset & Dunlap, Inc.

51 Madison Avenue   New York, N.Y. 10010

Published in the United States by Wonder Books, a Division
of Grosset & Dunlap, Inc.,

ISBN: 0-448-09669-2 (Trade Edition)
ISBN: 0-448-06389-1 (Library Edition)

FIRST PRINTING 1973

Printed and bound in the United States.

Library of Congress Catalog Card Number: 73-1977

This is a big farm.
A farmer lives here.
He lives in the farmhouse.

1

The farmer keeps cows.
These black and white cows
give a lot of milk.
2

The farmer uses machines
to milk the cows.

3

kale

Farmers grow food for their cows.
This farmer is growing kale.

4

hay-making in Switzerland

Cows eat hay in winter.
Hay is grass
dried in the sun.

5

This is a sheep farm.
Sheep eat grass.

6

electric shears

wool

Every spring
men cut the wool off the sheep.
This is called shearing.

7

bullock

beef joints

pork joints

pig

lamb

lamb joints

Some farmers keep animals for meat.
Different kinds of meat
come from different animals.

8

This farmer keeps hens.
The hens lay eggs
for people to eat.

9

barle

Any plant a farmer grows
is called a crop.
This farmer is growing barley.
Barley is a crop.
10

This farmer lives in France.
He is growing grapes.
He grows grapes
to make wine.

In some hot countries
people eat rice.
Farmers grow rice
in fields called paddy fields.
12

Some people keep fish to eat.
This place is a trout farm.
Trout are a kind of fish.

Some farmers grow fruit.
This farmer grows oranges.
14

cabbage

This farmer grows vegetables.
He has a big field of cabbages.
He grows potatoes, too.

15

This farmer is plowing a field.
A tractor is pulling the plow.
16

Where there is no tractor
animals pull the plow.
Horses pull plows.
Oxen pull plows.

When the field is plowed,
the farmer can sow seeds.
This farmer is sowing wheat.
18

When the wheat is ripe,
the farmer cuts it.
This is called the harvest.
This big farm is in Canada.

boll   flower

Here is a cotton field.
The cotton grows on bushes.
20

moth laying eggs

spinning

cocoons

chrysalis in a cocoon

caterpillar

This place is a silk farm.
Caterpillars like these
are kept here.
The caterpillars spin silk.

sugar cane

In the West Indies
farmers often grow sugar cane.
Sugar cane is used
to make sugar.

Starter's **Farms** words

farmer
(page 1)

hay
(page 5)

farmhouse
(page 1)

grass
(page 5)

cow
(page 2)

sheep
(page 6)

kale
(page 4)

hen
(page 9)

23

barley
(page 10)

wine
(page 11)

rice
(page 12)

trout
(page 13)

oranges
(page 14)

cabbage
(page 15)

potatoes
(page 15)

plow
(page 16)

tractor
(page 16)

horse
(page 17)

oxen
(page 17)

seed
(page 18)

wheat
(page 18)

cotton
(page 20)

silk
(page 21)

caterpillar
(page 21)

sugar cane
(page 22)

sugar
(page 22)

25

SISKIYOU COUNTY SCHOOLS
SCIENCE PROJECT